WHO WILL SAVE MY PLANET?

María Cristina Urrutia

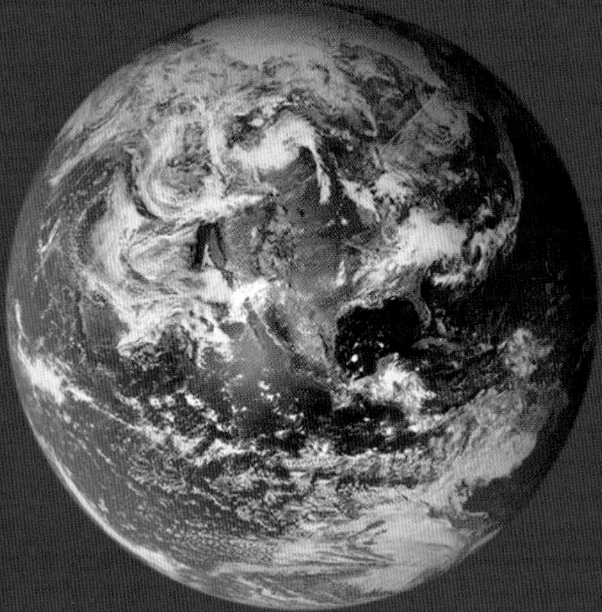

TUNDRA BOOKS

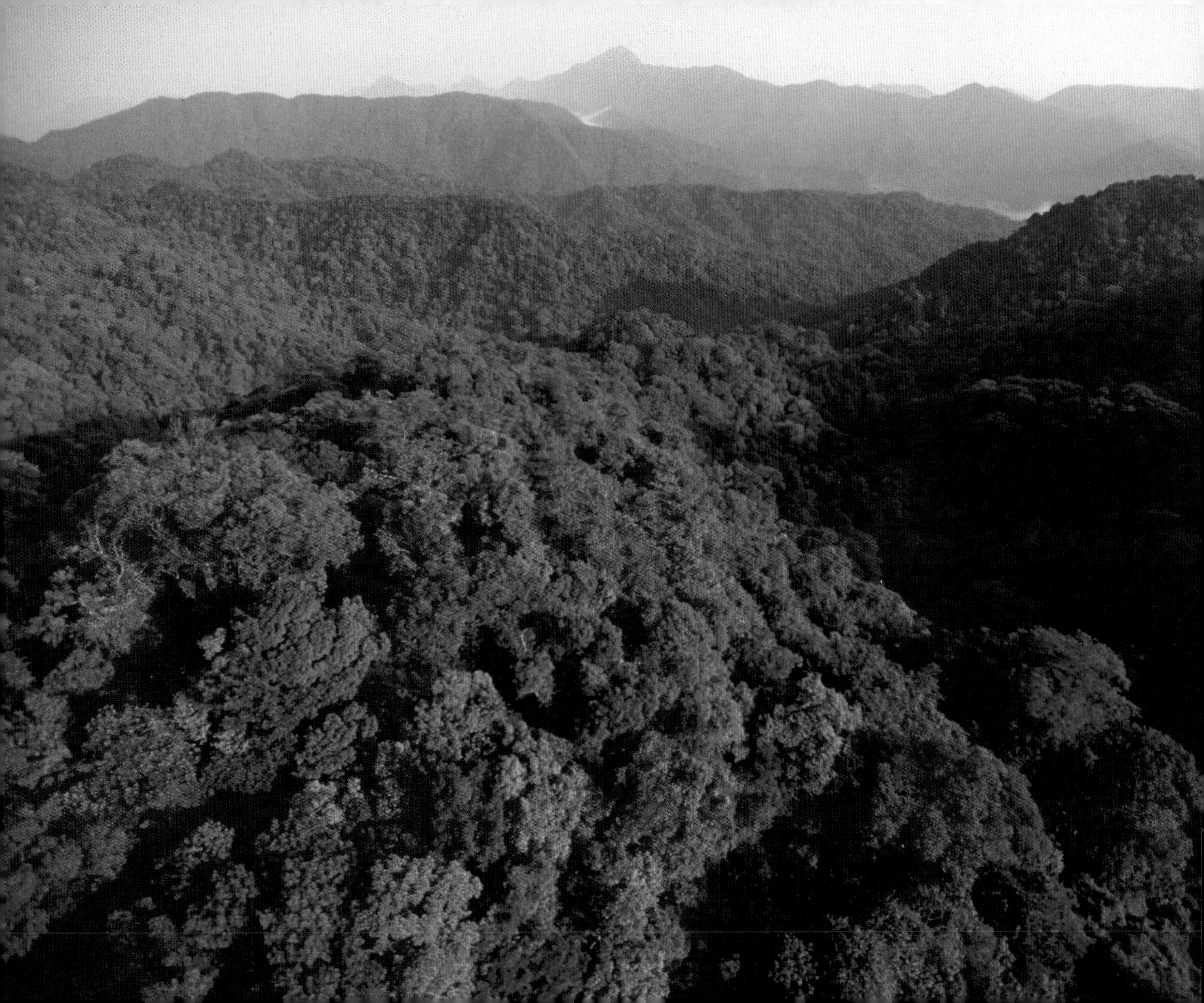

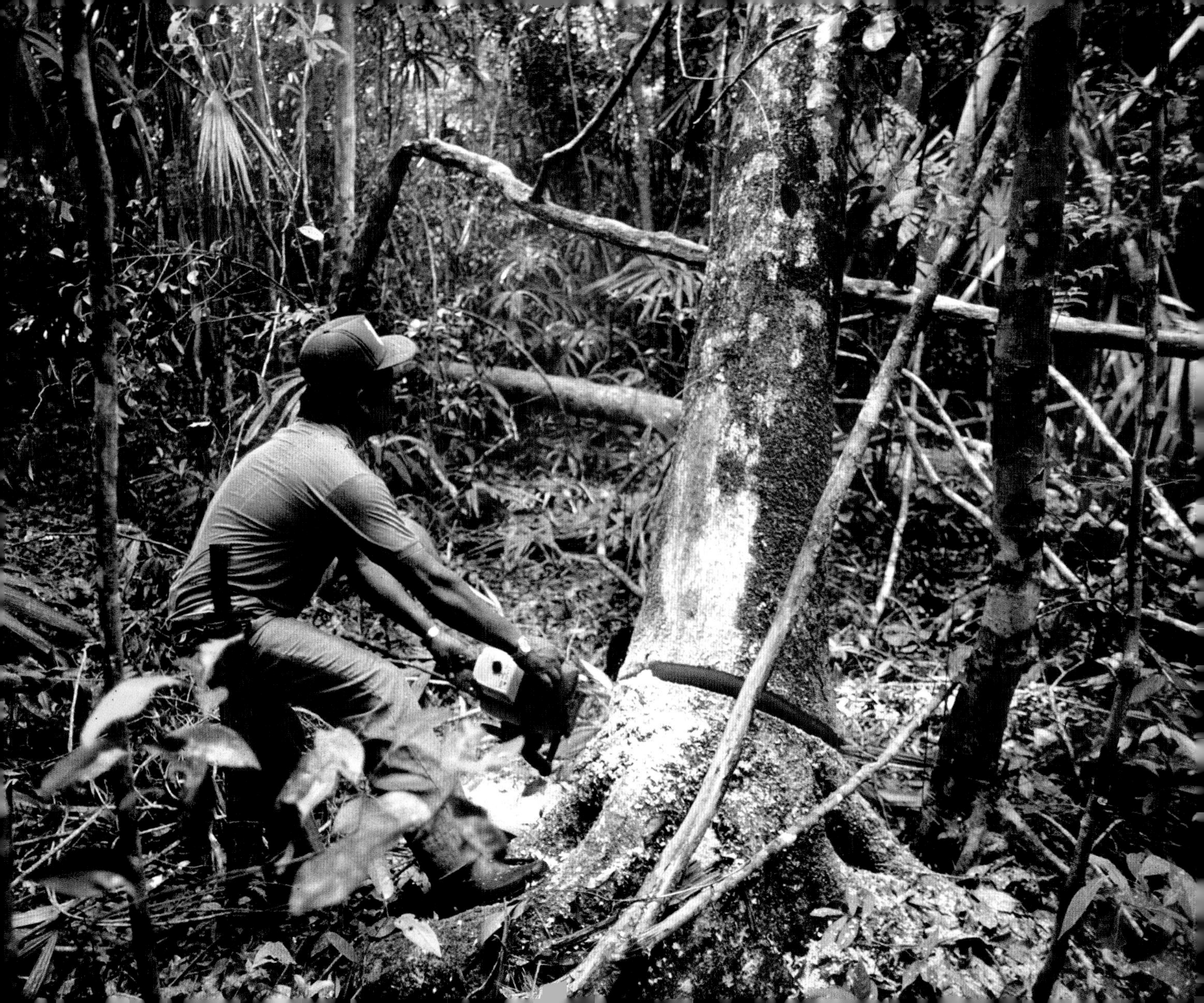

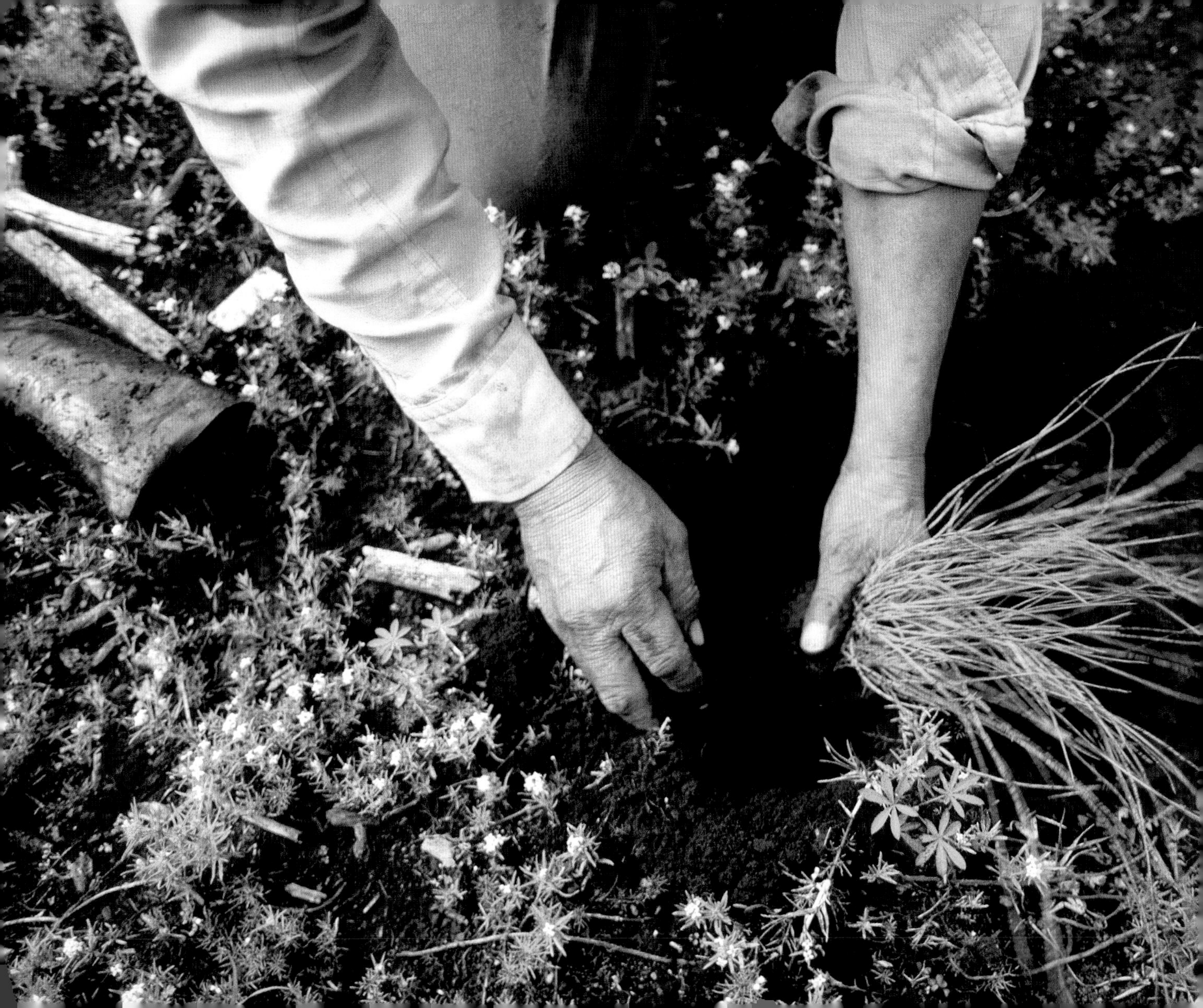

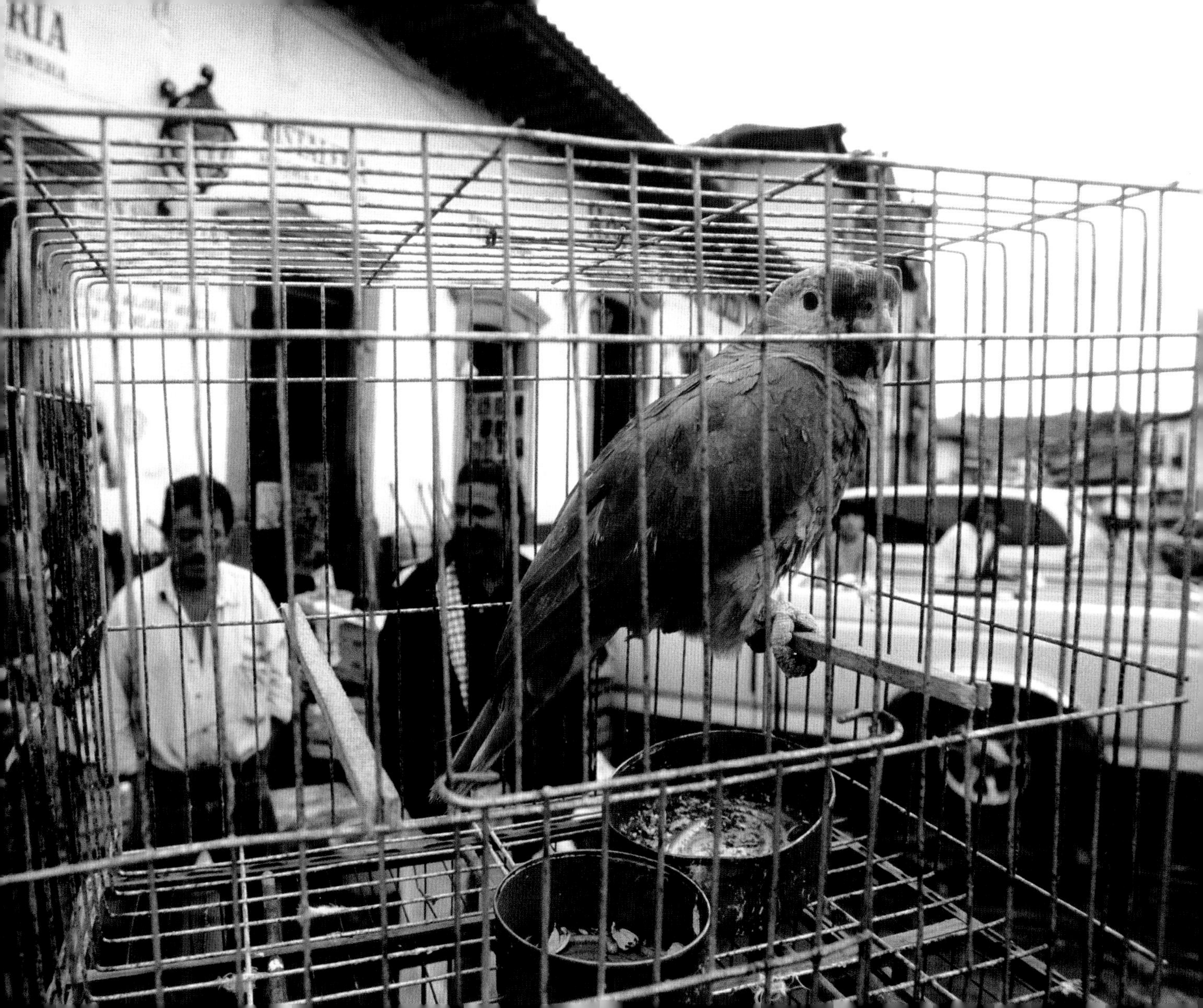
RIA

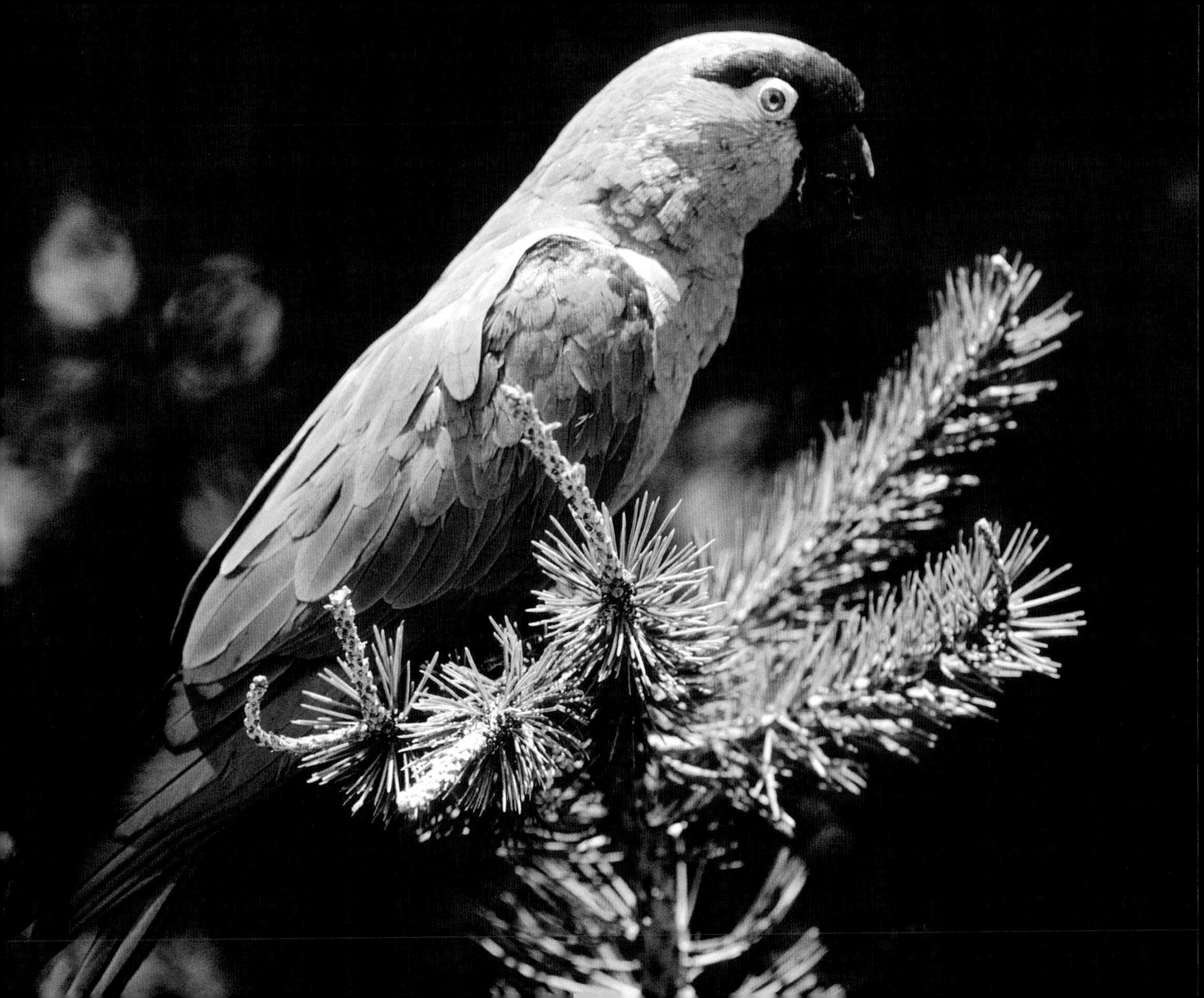

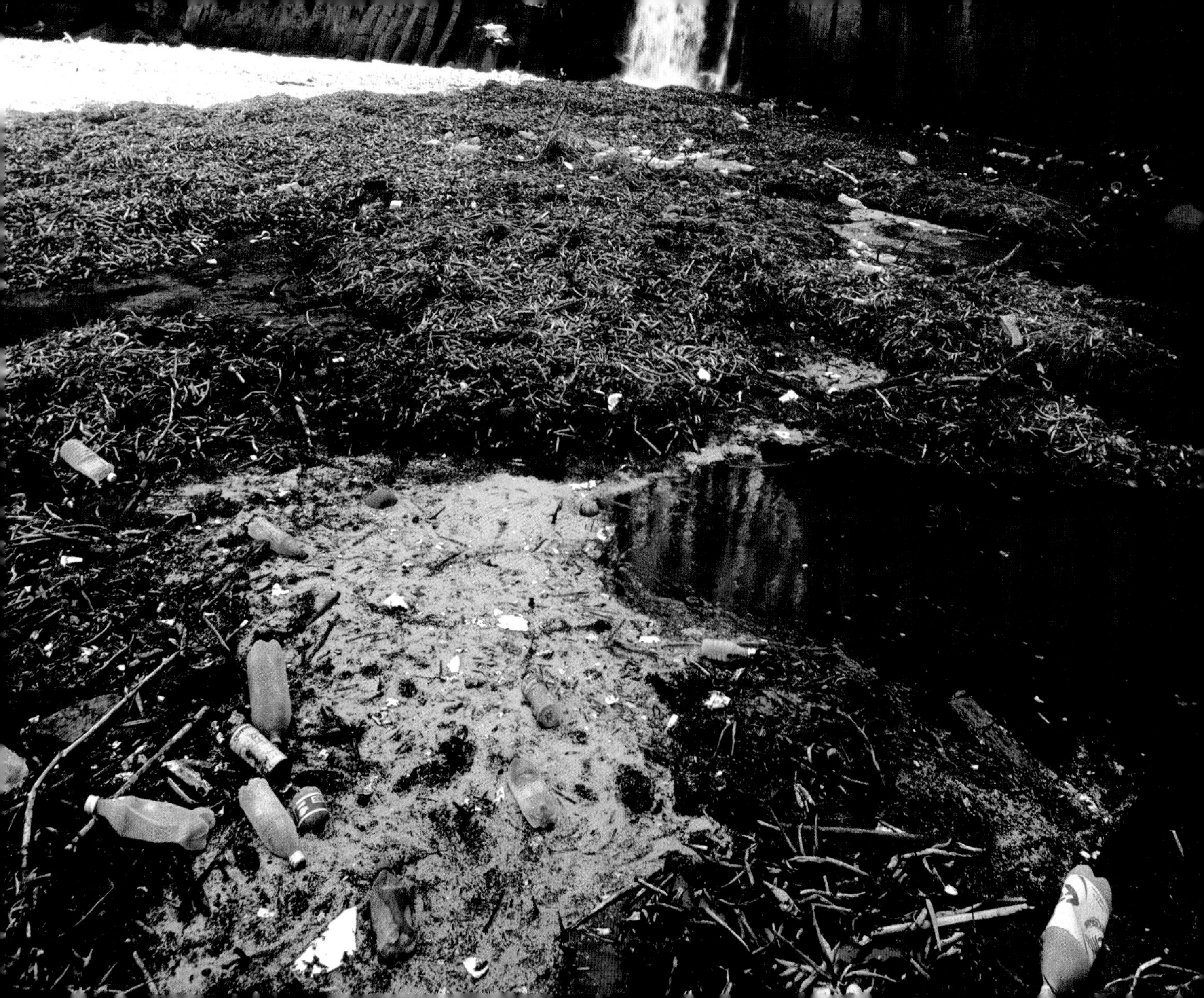

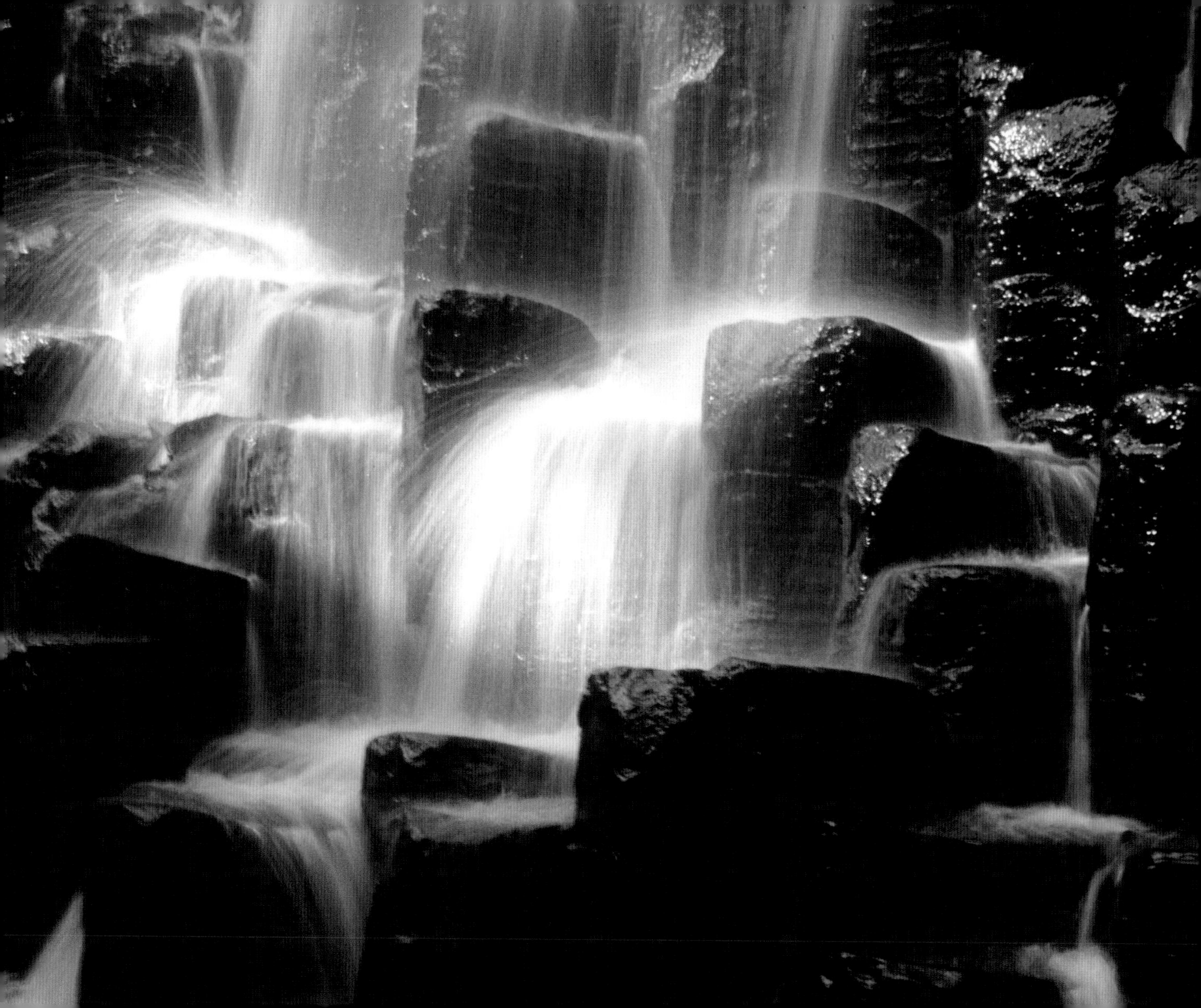

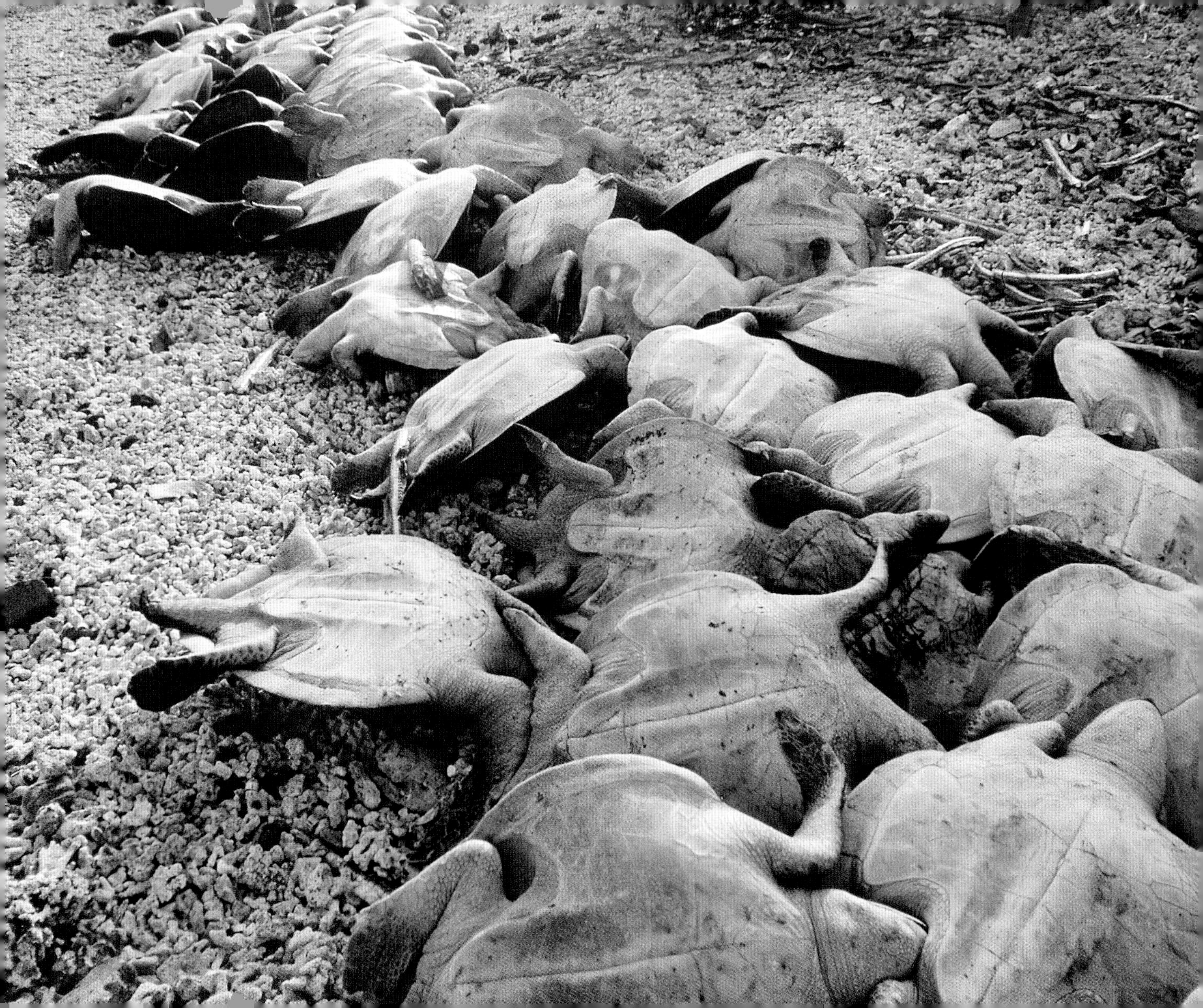

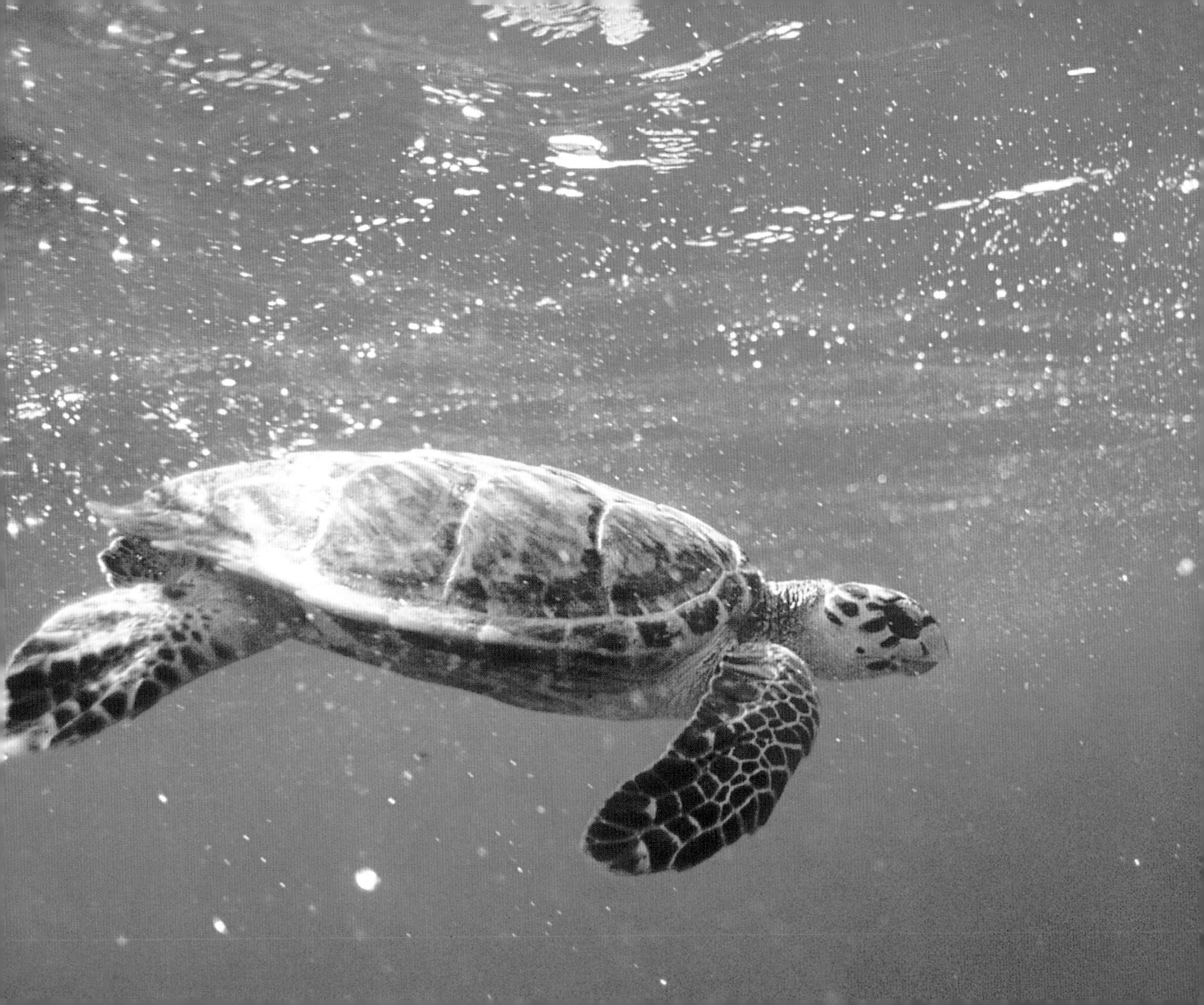

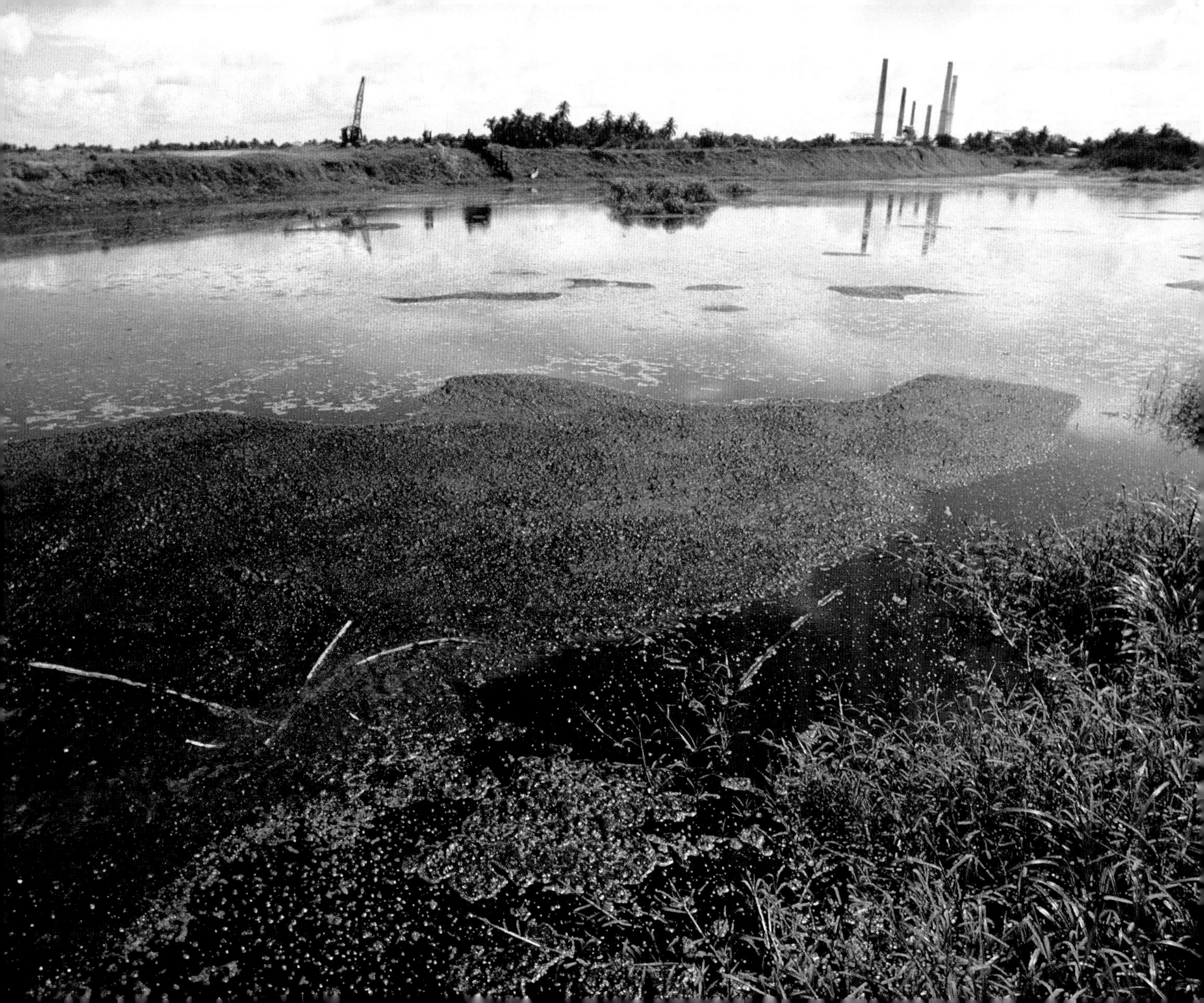

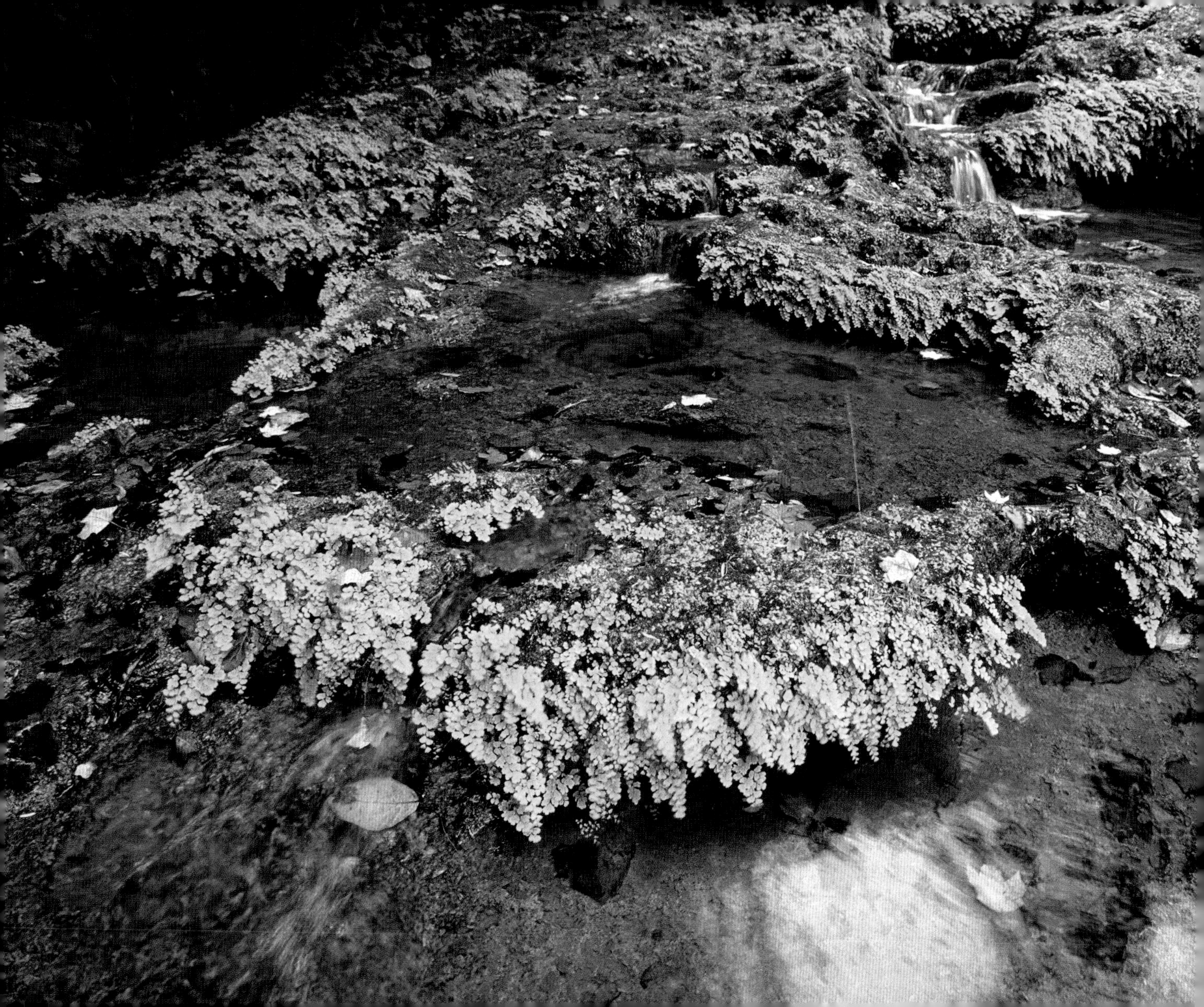

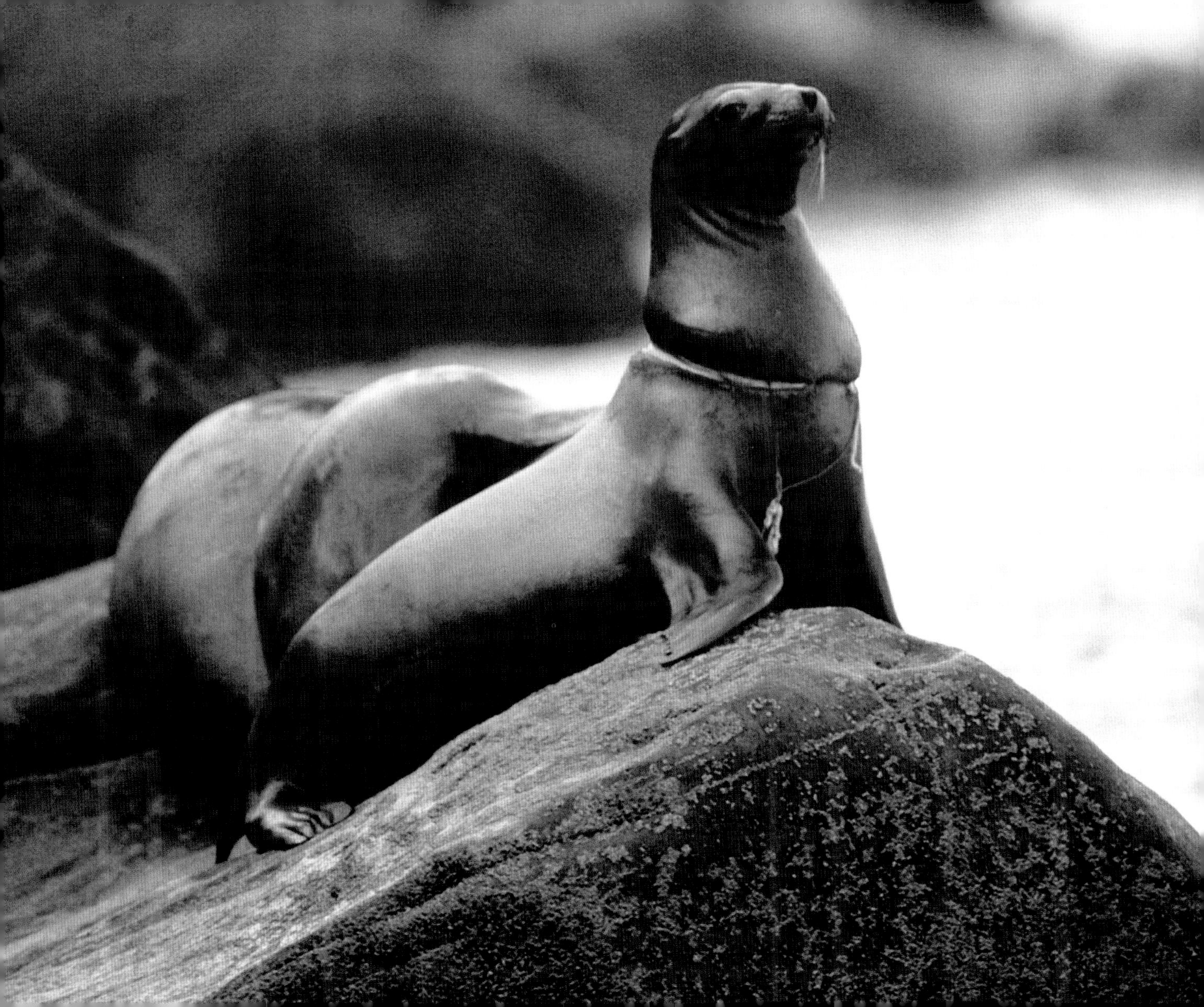

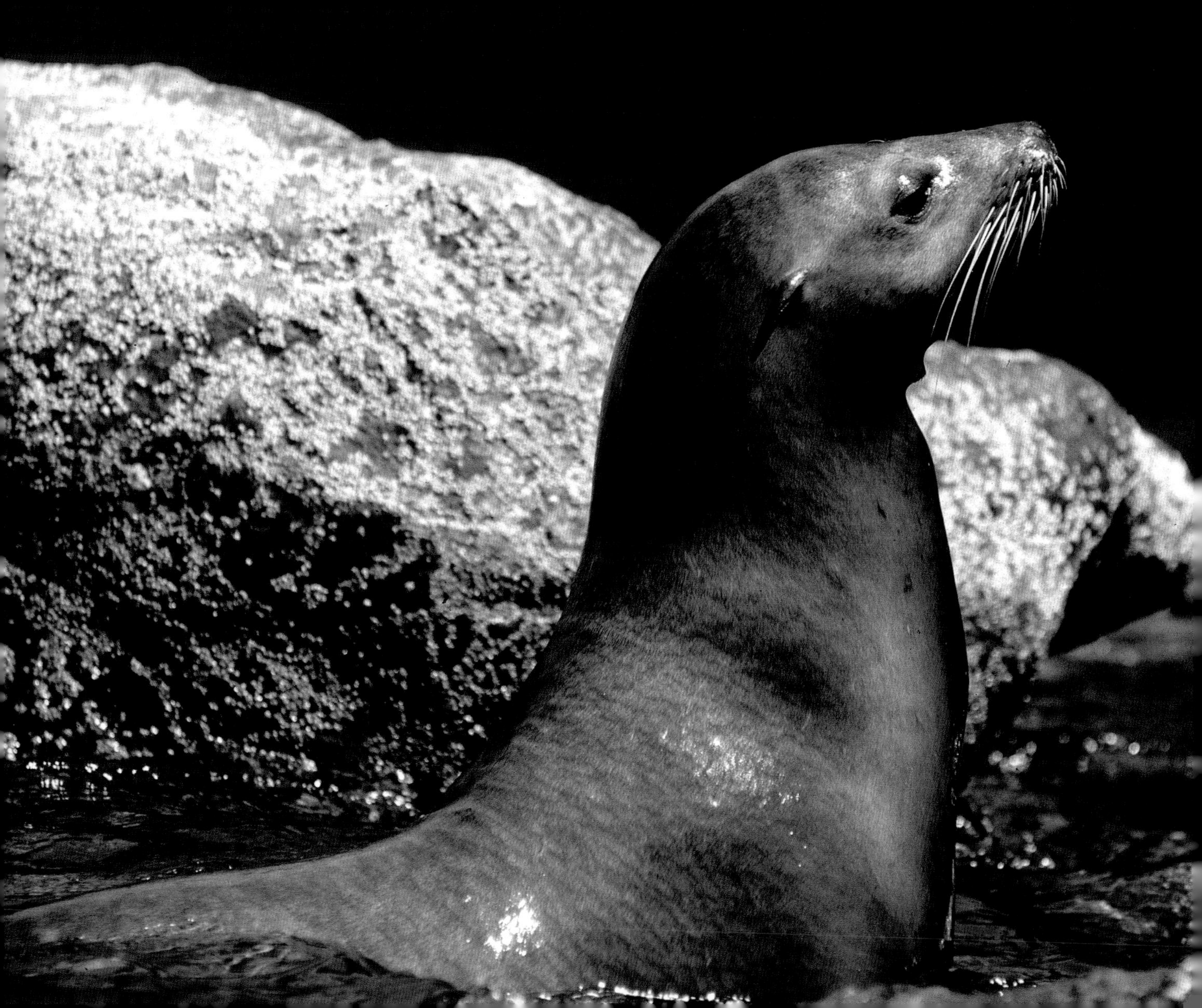

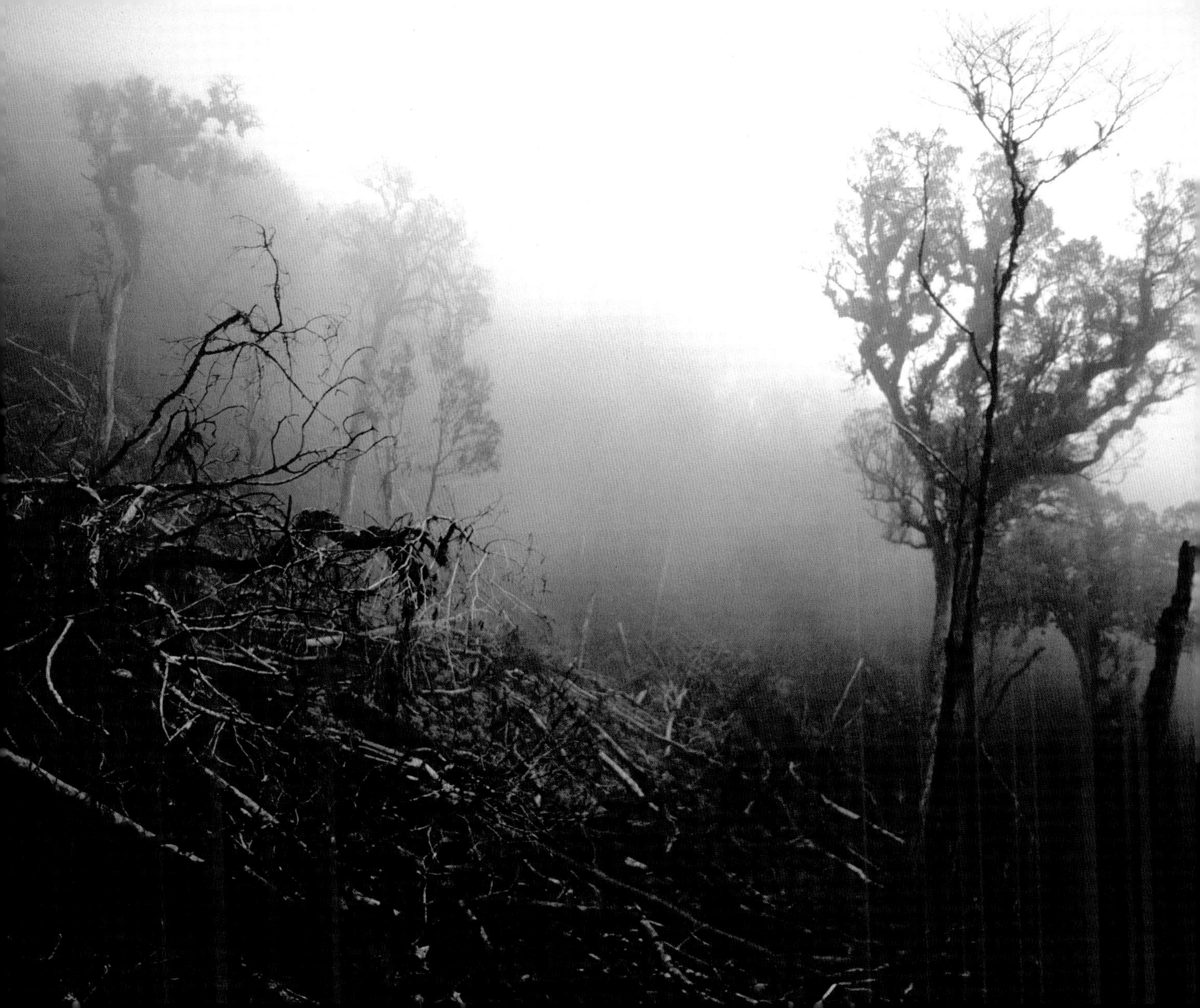

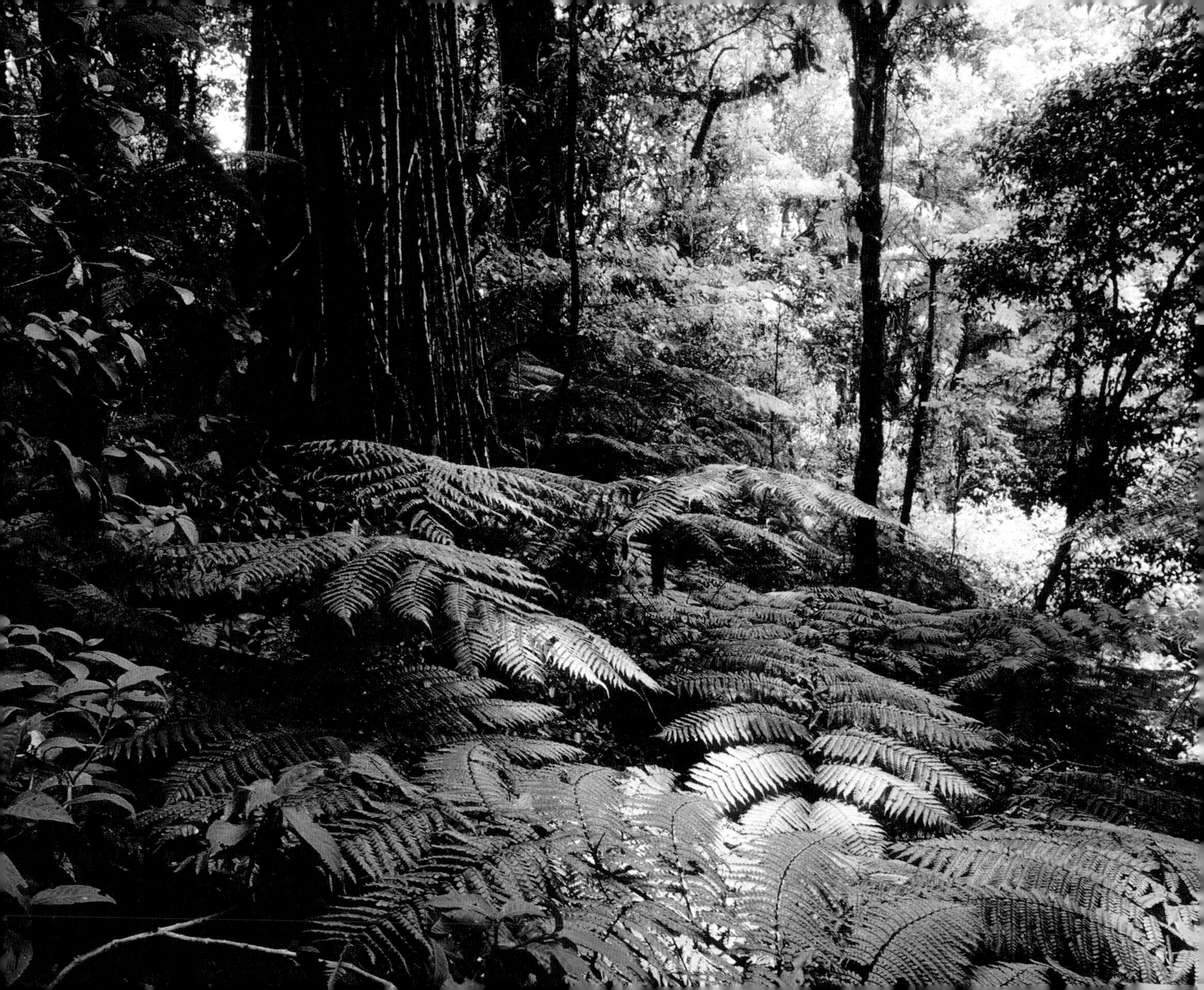

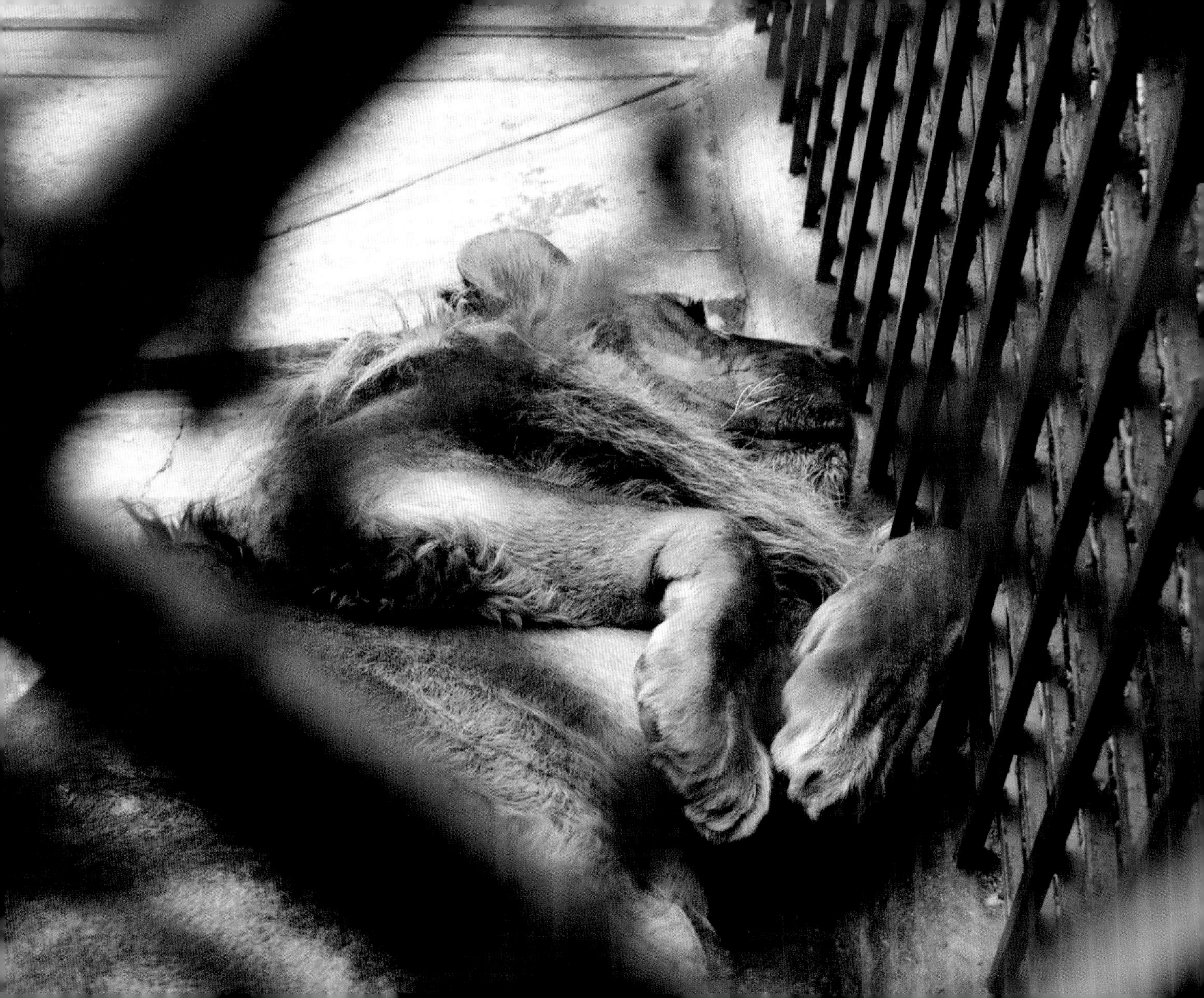

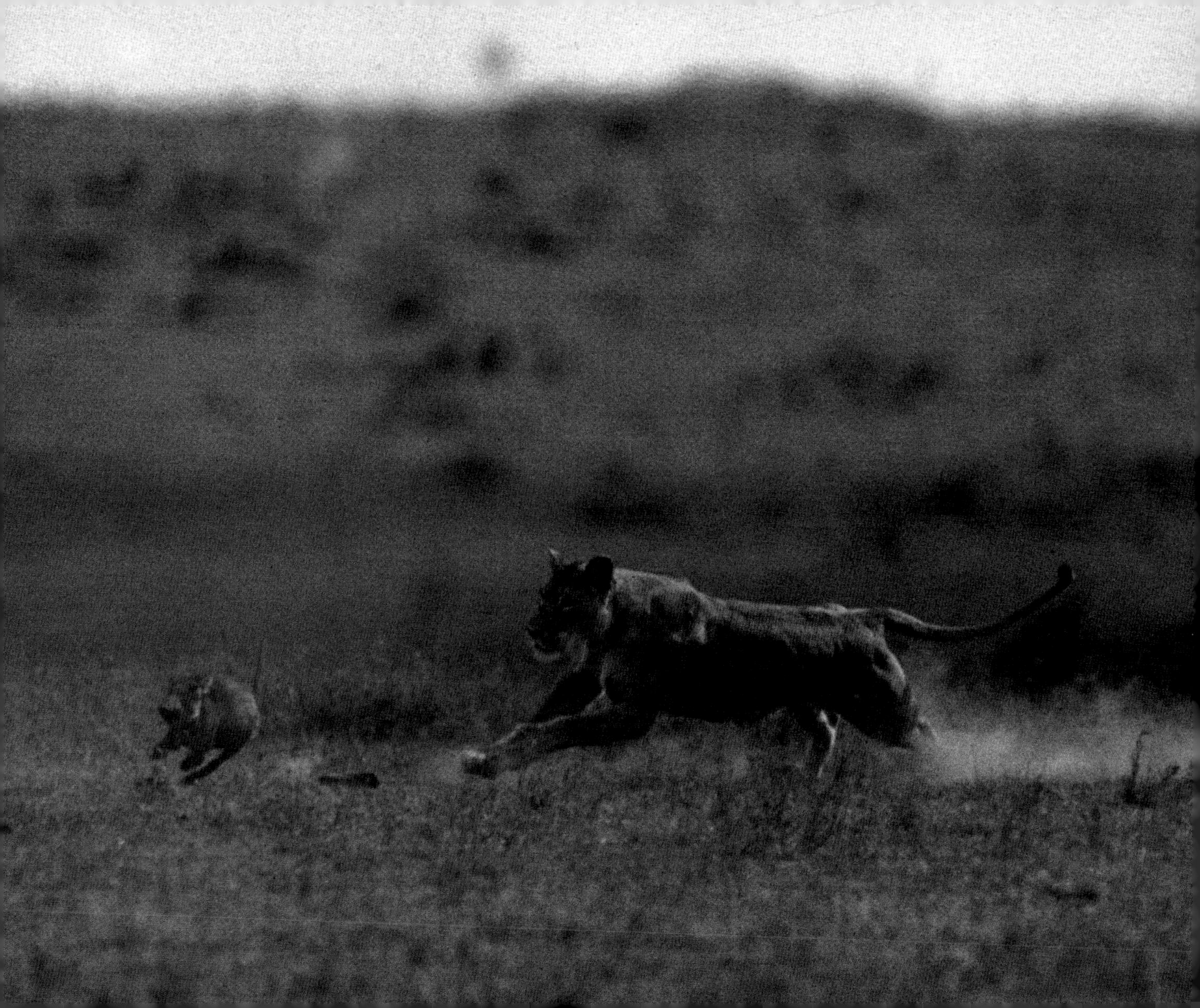

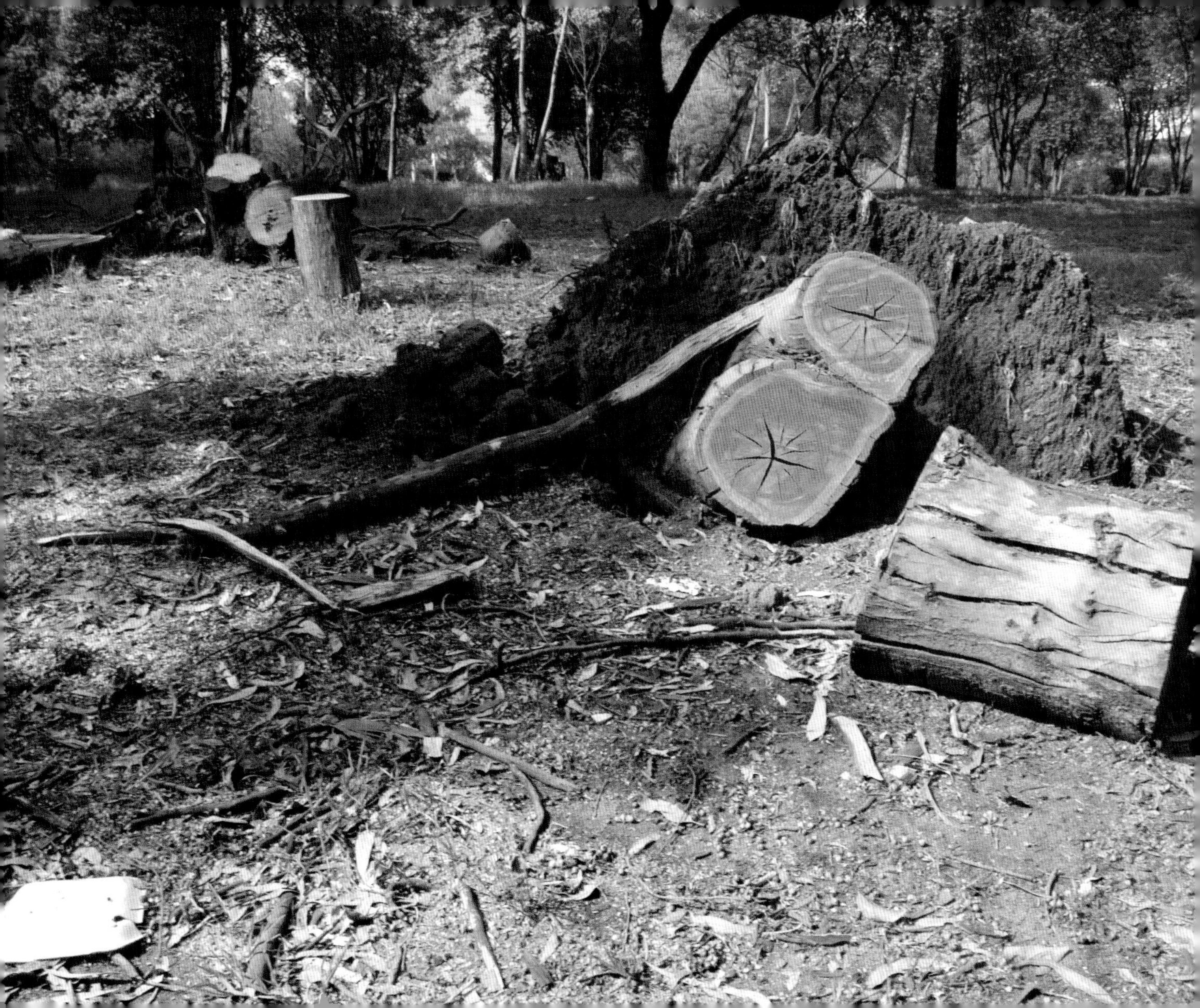

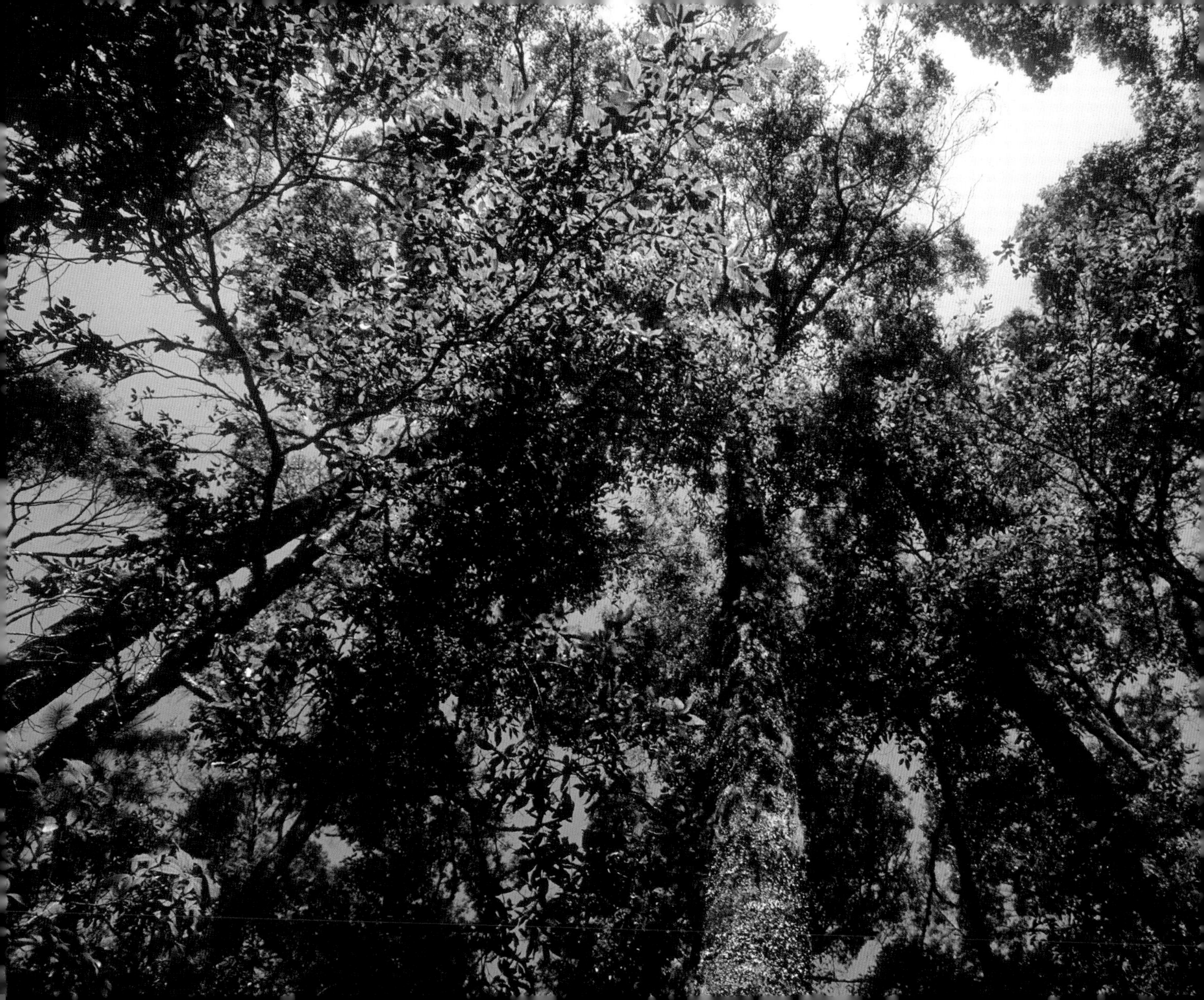

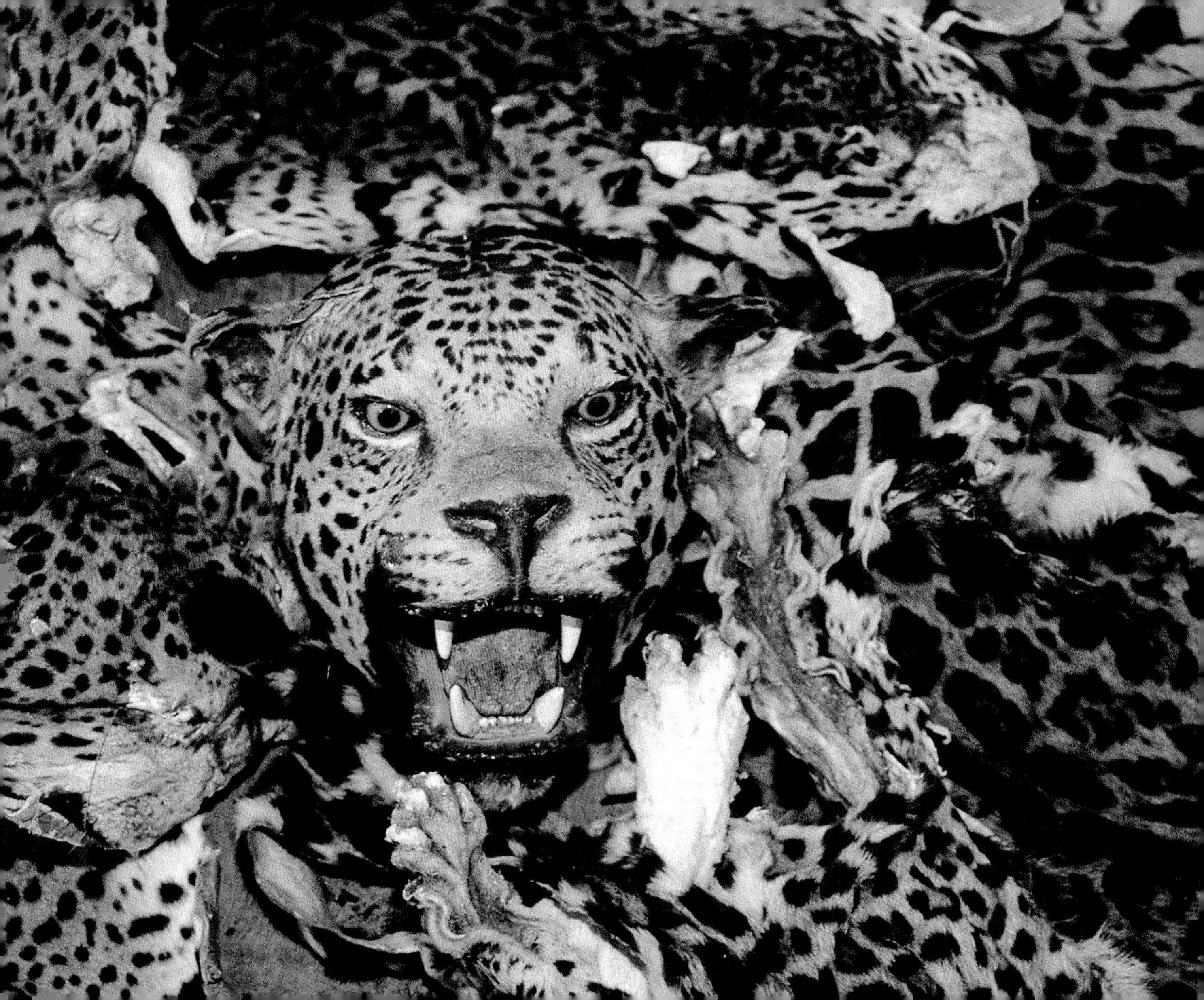

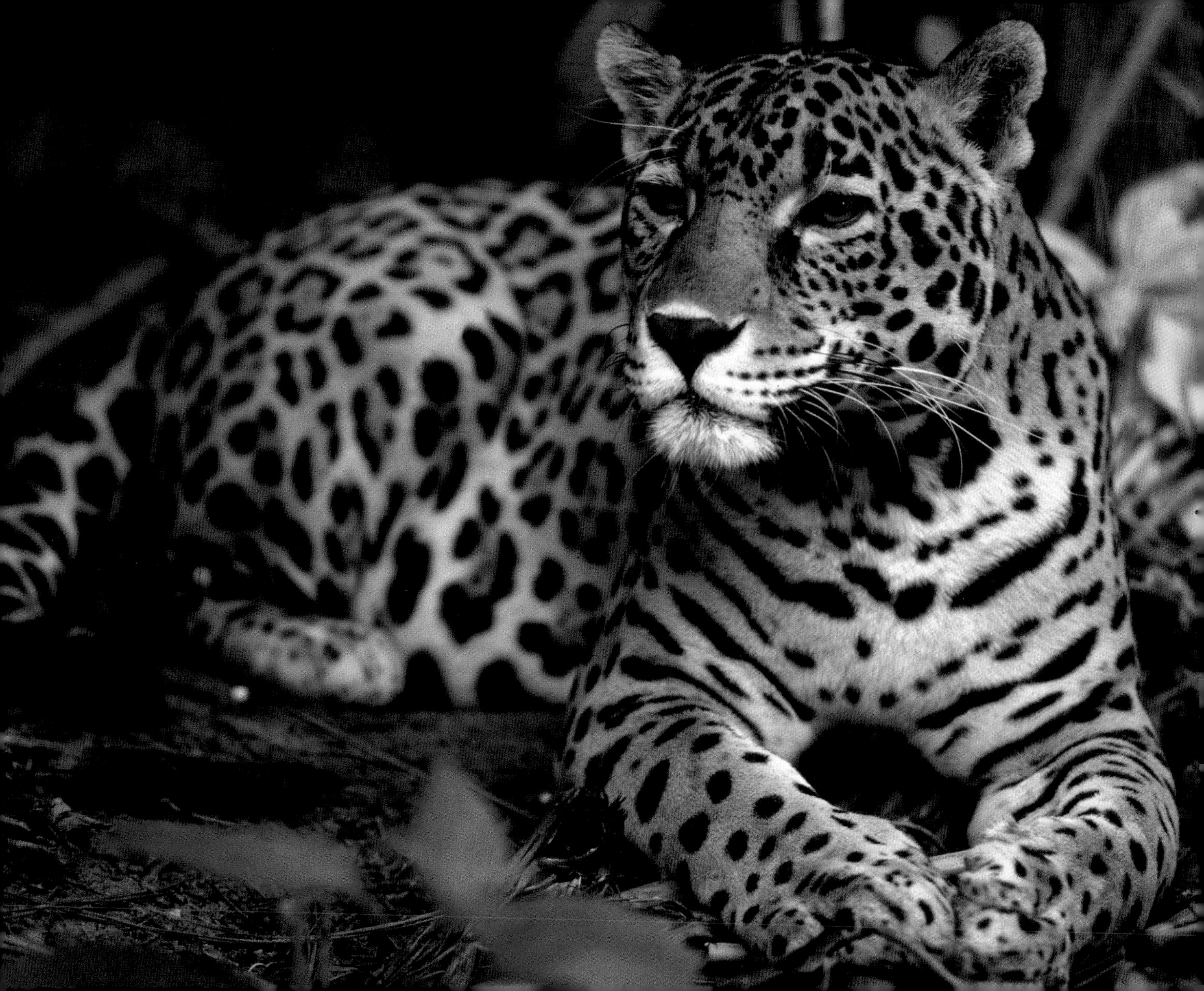

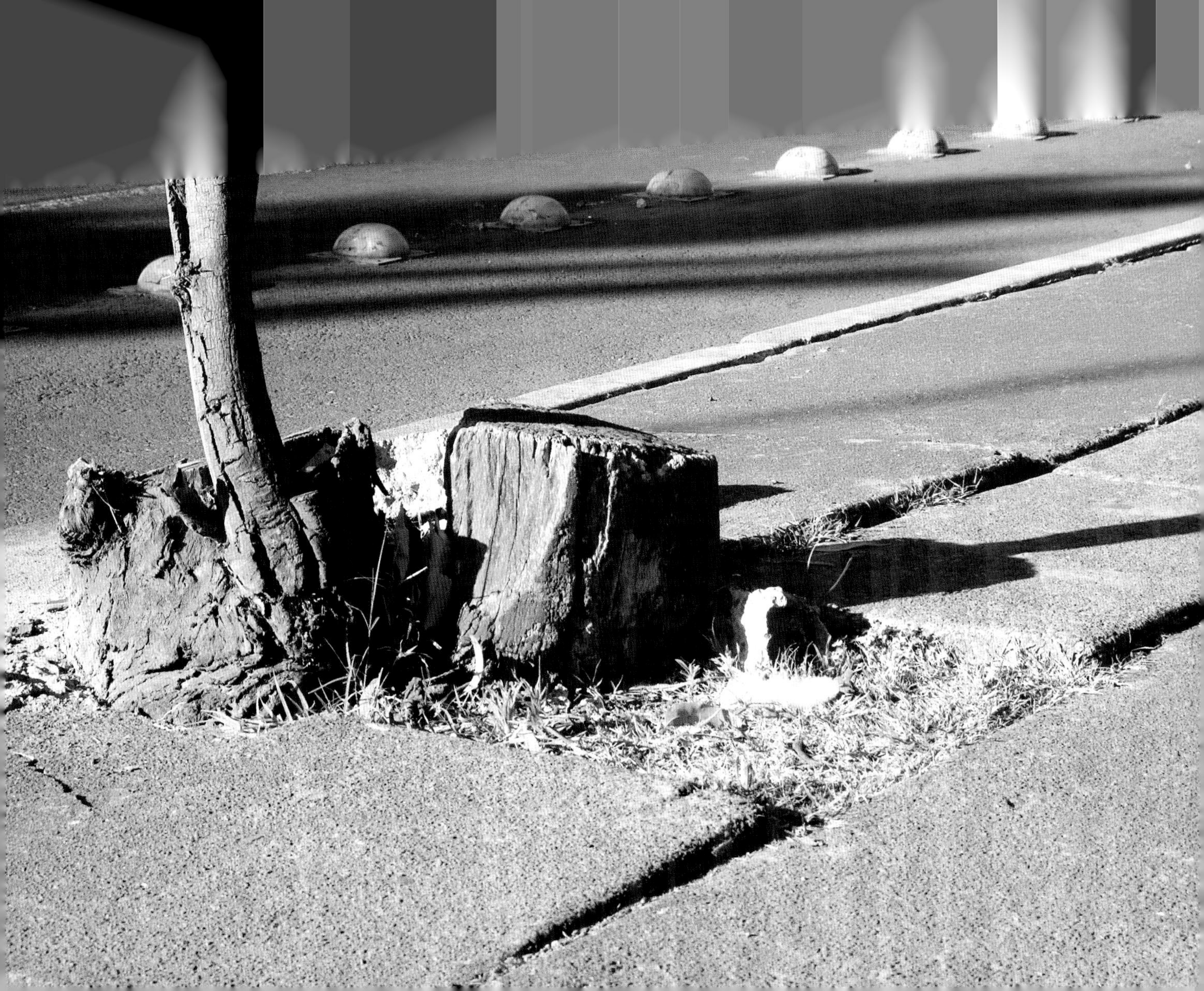

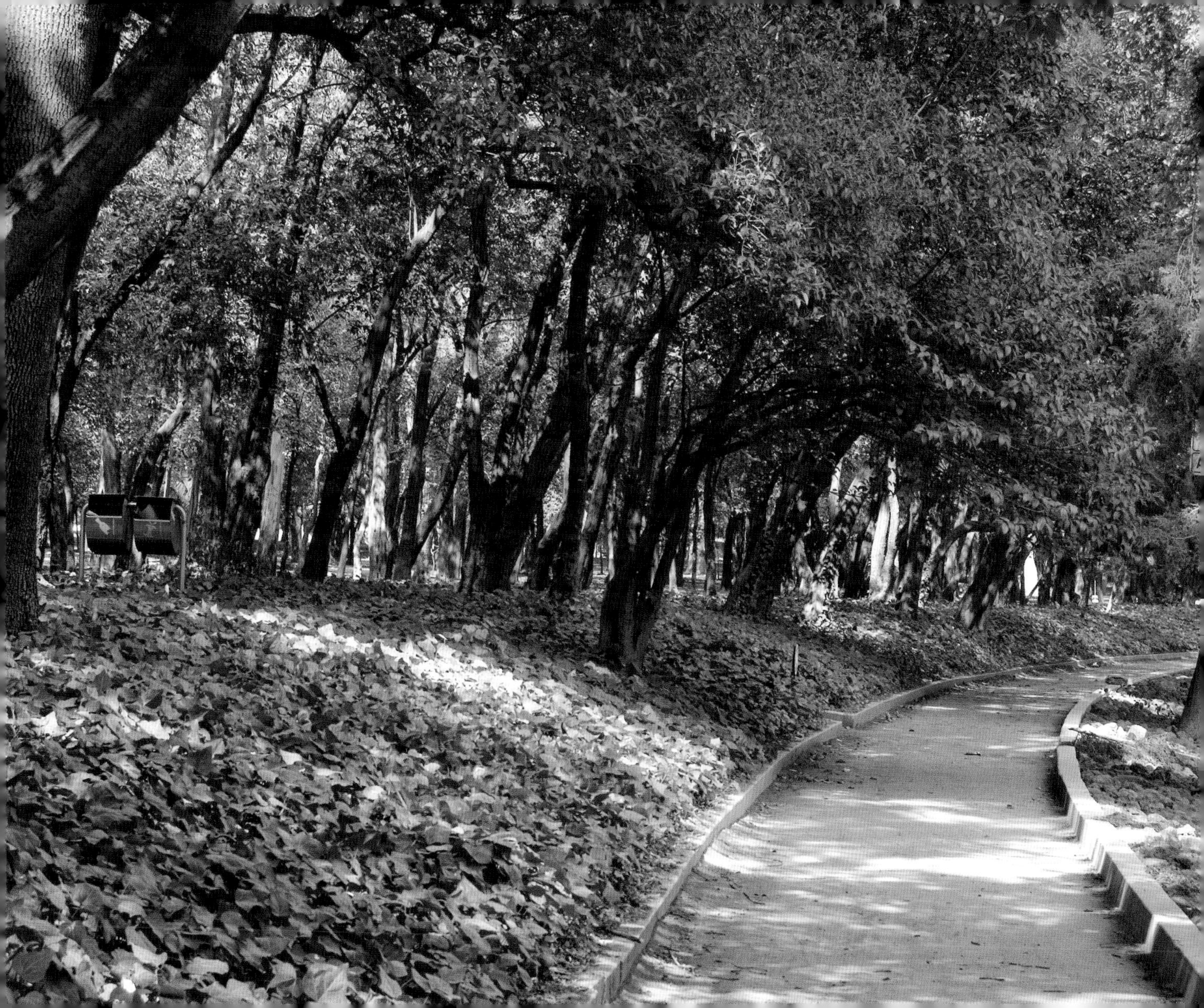

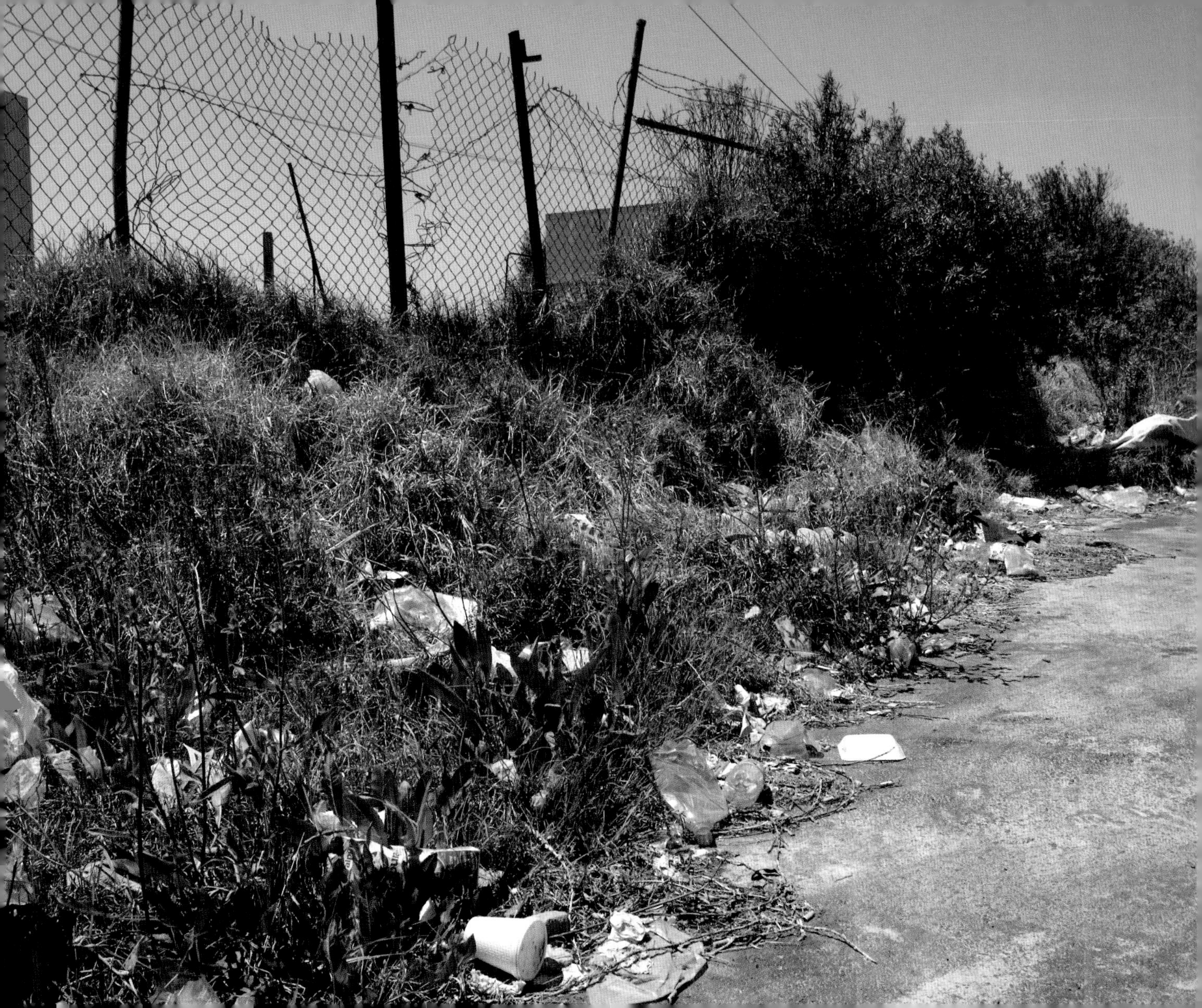

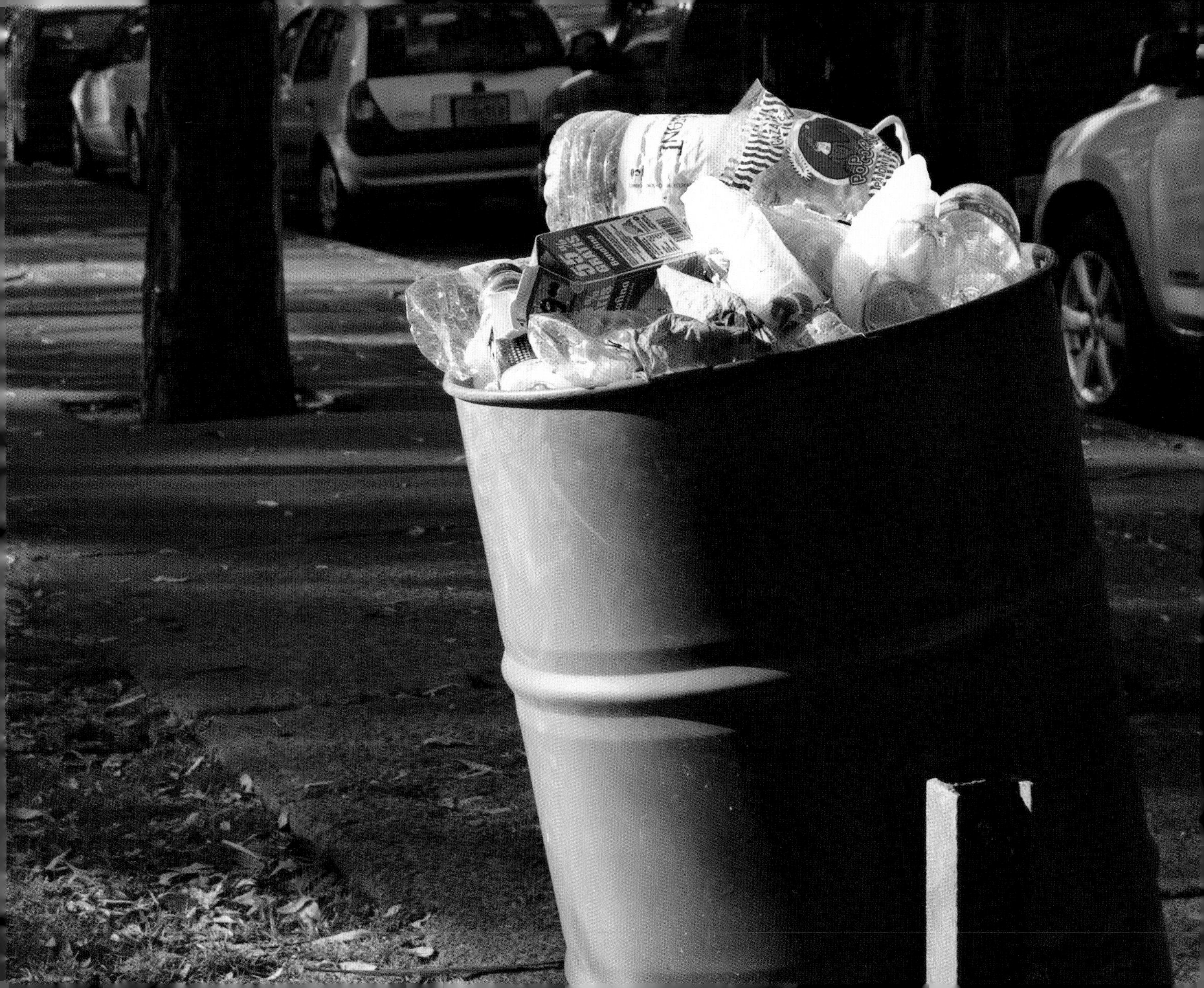

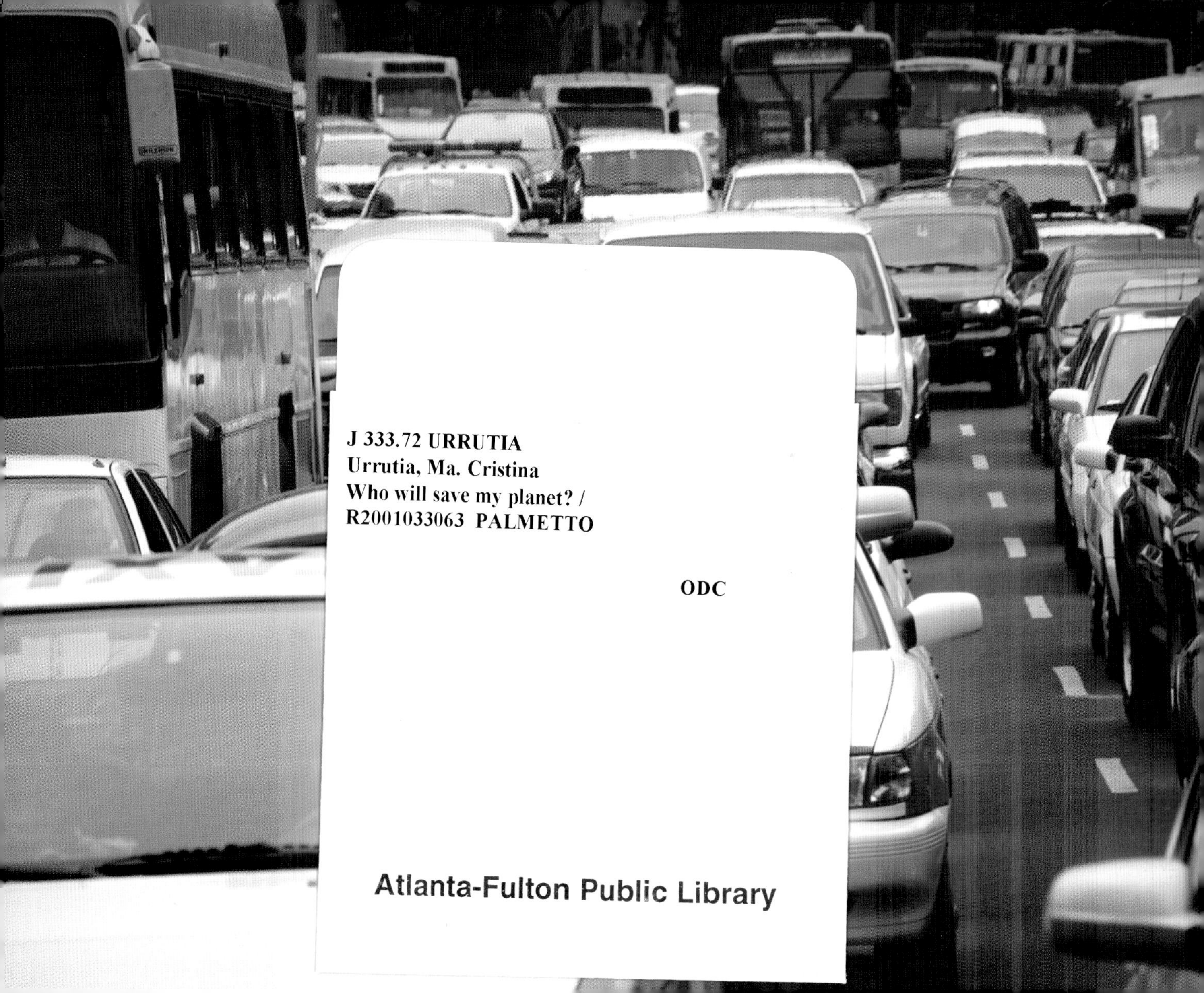